ISBN 978-1-331-99514-2
PIBN 10264881

This book is a reproduction of an important historical work. Forgotten Books uses
state-of-the-art technology to digitally reconstruct the work, preserving the original format
whilst repairing imperfections present in the aged copy. In rare cases, an imperfection in
the original, such as a blemish or missing page, may be replicated in our edition. We do,
however, repair the vast majority of imperfections successfully; any imperfections that
remain are intentionally left to preserve the state of such historical works.

1 MONTH OF
FREE
READING

at
www.ForgottenBooks.com

By purchasing this book you are eligible for one month membership to ForgottenBooks.com, giving you unlimited access to our entire collection of over 700,000 titles via our web site and mobile apps.

To claim your free month visit:

www.forgottenbooks.com/free264881

English
Français
Deutsche
Italiano
Español
Português

www.forgottenbooks.com

Mythology Photography **Fiction**
Fishing Christianity **Art** Cooking
Essays Buddhism Freemasonry
Medicine **Biology** Music **Ancient**
Egypt Evolution Carpentry Physics
Dance Geology **Mathematics** Fitness
Shakespeare **Folklore** Yoga Marketing
Confidence Immortality Biographies
Poetry **Psychology** Witchcraft
Electronics Chemistry History **Law**
Accounting **Philosophy** Anthropology
Alchemy Drama Quantum Mechanics
Atheism Sexual Health **Ancient History**
Entrepreneurship Languages Sport
Paleontology Needlework Islam
Metaphysics Investment Archaeology
Parenting Statistics Criminology
Motivational

Ambrose Bierce

By

Vincent Starrett

Chicago
Walter M. Hill
1920

THE TORCH PRESS
CEDAR RAPIDS
IOWA

TO
W. C. MORROW
AMBROSE BIERCE'S FRIEND AND MINE

ACKNOWLEDGEMENT

For valuable reminiscences and suggestions, extremely helpful in the preparation of this volume and its contents, I am indebted to many persons; particularly to W. C. Morrow, to Miss Carrie Christiansen, to Mrs. Josephine Clifford McCrackin, to Helen Bierce Isgrigg, and to Walter Neale, Major Bierce's publisher. I am happy here to give public utterance to my gratitude. A number of characteristic anecdotes are quoted from Bierce's autobiographic vignettes, in his "Collected Works."

V. S.

NOTE

More than six years of speculation and apprehension have passed since the disappearance of Ambrose Bierce. Sanguine hopes long have dwindled, and only the frailest possibility survives that he yet lives in some green recess of the Mexican mountains, or some tropical Arcadia in South America. Assuming that he is dead, as we must assume who do not look for a miracle, he has fulfilled a prophecy made years ago by a writing man of his acquaintance:

"Some day he will go up on Mount Horeb and forget to come down. No man will see his death-struggle, for he'll cover his face with his cloak of motley, and if he sends a wireless it will be this: ' 'Tis a grave subject.' "

There has been no wireless.

In the circumstances, it is perhaps presumptuously early to attempt an estimate of the man and his work; but already both fools and angels have rushed in, and the atmosphere is thick with rumor and legend. The present appraisal, at least is not fortuitous, and its stated facts have the merit of sobriety and authority.

I. THE MAN

There are many persons who do not care for the writings of Ambrose Bierce, and thousands — it is shocking to reflect — who never have heard of him. The Hon. Franklin K. Lane, erstwhile Secretary of the Interior, has gone on record as thinking him "a hideous monster, so like the mixture of dragon, lizard, bat, and snake as to be unnameable," a characterization almost Biercian in its cumulative invective. When Mr. Lane made this remark, or wrote it down (whichever may have been the case), he said it with pious horror and intense dislike; but when Gertrude Atherton asserted that Bierce had the most brutal imagination she had encountered in print, she was paying him a compliment, and she intended to. Out of those two appraisals we may extract the truth — that Bierce was a mighty artist in his field, with little or no concern for the reactions of weaker vessels to his art.

A great many persons knew Ambrose Bierce, and some loved him, and some hated and feared him. All, from their own point of view, had excellent reason for their quality of regard. Save for those who made up this catholic and vari-minded assemblage, few persons can speak of Ambrose Bierce, the man. The story of Ambrose Bierce the novelist, the satirist, the humorist, and the poet, is to a large degree the story of Ambrose Bierce the man; but to a larger degree is the story of Ambrose Bierce the man the story of Ambrose Bierce the novelist, satirist, humorist, and poet.

It is generally known that he served throughout the Civil War. He emerged a Major, brevetted for distinguished services, and with an honorable scar upon his body. Twice he had rescued wounded comrades from the battlefield, at the risk of his life; at Kenesaw Mountain he was severely wounded in the head. He came out of the conflict a soldier, with a decided leaning toward literature, and the story goes that he tossed up a coin to determine his career. Instead of "head" or "tail" he may have called "sword" or "pen," but the story does not so inform us. Whatever the deciding influence may have been, Bierce commenced journalist and author in San Francisco, in 1866, as editor of the *News Letter*. Then, in 1872, he went to London, where, for four years, or until 1876, he was on the staff of *Fun*, edited by the younger Tom Hood.

In London, the editors of *Fun*, amazed at the young man's fertile ability, conceived the notion that he could write anything, and accordingly piled his desk with a weird assortment of old woodcuts, minus their captions; they requested that he "write

things" to fit them. The "things" Bierce wrote
astonished England, and Pharisees squirmed beneath
his lash as they had not done since the days of Swift.
A cruel finger was on secret ulcers, and the American's satires quickly gained for him, among his col-
leagues, the name of "Bitter Bierce." The stinging
tales and fables he produced to order are those
found in the volume called *Cobwebs From an
Empty Skull*, reputed to be by Dod Grile, and published in 1874. A year previously, he had published
The Fiend's Delight, and *Nuggets and Dust*, caustic
little volumes largely made up of earlier diabolisms
from California journals. His intimates of the
period included such joyous spirits as Hood, George
Augustus Sala, and Capt. Mayne Reid, the boys'
novelist; this quartette, with others, frequented a
taproom in Ludgate Station, and gave itself over, as
Bierce humorously confesses, "to shedding the blood
of the grape."

Thus Bierce:

> We worked too hard, dined too well, fre-
> quented too many clubs and went to bed too
> late in the forenoon. In short, we diligently,
> conscientiously and with a perverse satisfaction
> burned the candle of life at both ends and in
> the middle.

He relates some delightful episodes of the period
in his *Bits of Autobiography*, the first volume in his
Collected Works; the funniest and one of the most

typical, perhaps, is that concerning his difficulties with John Camden Hotten, a publisher with whom Mark Twain was having trouble of his own at about the same time — although at a greater distance.   Hotten owed Bierce money for certain work, and Bierce, usually financially embarrassed, hounded Hotten for it until the publisher, in despair, sent the implacable creditor to negotiate with his (Hotten's) manager.   Bierce talked vividly for two hours, at the end of which time the crestfallen manager capitulated and produced a check already made out and signed.   It bore date of the following Saturday.   The rest of the story belongs to Bierce:

Before Saturday came, Hotten proceeded to die of a pork pie in order to beat me out of my money.   Knowing nothing of this, I strolled out to his house in Highgate, hoping to get an advance, as I was in great need of cash.   On being told of his demise I was inexpressibly shocked, for my cheque was worthless.   There was a hope, however, that the bank had not heard.   So I called a cab and drove furiously bank-ward. Unfortunately my gondolier steered me past Ludgate Station, in the bar whereof our Fleet Street gang of writers had a private table.   I disembarked for a mug of bitter.   Unfortunately, too, Sala, Hood, and others of the gang were in their accustomed places.   I sat at board and related the sad event.   The deceased had not in life enjoyed our favour, and I blush to say we all fell to making questionable epi-

taphs to him. I recall one by Sala which ran
thus:

Hotten,
Rotten,
Forgotten.

At the close of the rites, several hours later, I
resumed my movements against the bank. Too
late — the old story of the hare and the tor-
toise was told again! The heavy news had
overtaken and passed me as I loitered by the
wayside. I attended the funeral, at which I
felt more than I cared to express.

The appearance of his *Cobwebs From an Empty
Skull* made Bierce for a time the chief wit and humorist of England, and, combined with his satirical
work on *Fun*, brought about his engagement by
friends of the exiled Empress Eugénie to conduct a
journal against her enemies, who purposed to make
her refuge in England untenable by newspaper attacks. It appeared that James Mortimer, who was
later to found and edit the *Figaro*, was in the habit
of visiting the exiled Empress at Chislehurst, and
he it was who learned of a threat by M. Henri
Rochefort to start his paper, *La Lanterne*, in England; Rochefort, who had persistently attacked the
Empress in Paris. Mortimer suggested the found-
ing and registering in London of a paper called *The
Lantern*, which was done and Bierce was made its
editor. But the struggle never came; Rochefort,
outwitted, knew the game was up, and did not put

his threat into execution, although Bierce, for a few numbers, had the delight of abusing the Frenchman to his heart's content, a pursuit he found extremely congenial.

Bierce the satirist was for a time in his element; but there was little material wealth to be gained in London, and at times he was pretty hard up. He revived his failing fortunes for a short period by writing and publishing his series of "Little Johnny" stories — humorous, misspelled essays in zoölogy, supposed to be the work of a small boy. These were popular and added color to his name; but Bierce's mind was now turning backward to the country he had deserted, and in 1876 he returned to San Francisco.

He remained then on the coast for a quarter of a century, save for a brief period of mining near Deadwood, South Dakota, where his adventures with road-agents and other bad men were hair-raising. On a night in 1880 he was driving in a light wagon through a wild part of the Black Hills. The wagon carried thirty thousand dollars in gold belonging to the mining company of which he was manager, and beside him on the wagon seat was Boone May, a famous gunman who was under in-dictment for murder. May had been paroled on Bierce's promise that he would see him into custody again. The notorius gunman sat, huddled in his rubber poncho, with his rifle between his knees; he was acting as guard of the company's gold. Although Bierce thought him somewhat *off* guard, he said nothing.

There came a sudden shout: "Throw up your hands!"

Bierce reached for his revolver, but it was needless. Almost before the words had left the highwayman's lips, with the quickness of a cat May had hurled himself backward over the seat, face upward, and with the muzzle of his weapon within a yard of the bandit's throat, had fired a shot that forever ruined the interrupter's usefulness as a road-agent.

Bierce returned again to San Francisco. Through the warp and woof, then, of certain California journals, for many years, ran the glittering thread of his genius, and to this period belongs much of his finest and strongest work. He became a mighty censor who made and unmade men and women, a Warwick of the pen. It is no exaggeration to say that corrupt politicians, hypocritical philanthropists and clergymen, self-worshipers, notoriety seekers, and pretenders of every description trembled at his name. He wielded an extraordinary power; his pen hung, a Damoclean sword, over the length and breadth of the Pacific coast. Those who had cause to fear his wrath opened their morning papers with something like horror. He wrote "epitaphs" to persons not yet dead, of such a nature — had they been dead — as to make them turn in their graves. Many of his poetic quips were venomous to a degree, and he greeted Oscar Wilde, on the poet's arrival in America, in 1882, with a blast of invective that all but paralyzed that ready wit. His pet abominations were James Whitcomb Riley and Ella Wheeler Wilcox. In the earlier days of his power an assault in print was believed sufficient cause for a pistoled reply, and Bierce was always a marked man; but he was utterly fearless, and as he was known to be a dead shot, himself, his life always was "spared" by the victims of his attacks. His vocabulary of invective was the widest and most vitriolic of any modern journalist, but it was not billingsgate; Bierce never penned a line that was not impeccable. His wit was diabolic — Satanic — but he was always the scholar, and he always bowed politely before he struck. The suave fierceness of his attack is unique in contemporaneous literature.

He cherished no personal enmities, in the ordinary sense, for his attacks were largely upon principles promoted by men, rather than upon the men themselves. One who knew him once said: "I look upon Bierce as a literary giant. I don't think he really means to walk rough-shod over people, any more than a lion means to be rough with a mouse. It is only that the lion wonders how anything so small can be alive, and he is amused by its antics." With his clairvoyant vision, his keen sense of justice, and his extraordinary honesty, what an international fool-killer he would have made!

Yet this fierce and hated lampooner had his softer side, which he displayed to those he loved and who loved him; and these were not too few. One of his oldest friends writes, in a letter: "His private gentleness, refinement, tenderness, kindness, unselfishness, are my most cherished memories of him. He was deeply — I may say childishly — human. . . It was in these intimate things, the aspects which the world never saw, that he made himself so deeply loved by the few whom he held close. For he was exceedingly reserved. Under no circumstances could he ever be dragged into physical view before the crowds that hated, feared or admired him. He had no vanity; his insolence toward the mob was detached, for he was an aristocrat to the bottom of him. But he would have given his coat to his bitterest enemy who happened to be cold."

His humor, as distinct from his wit, was queer and picturesque, and was a distinguished quality. In his column of "Prattle" in the *San Francisco Examiner*, he once remarked that something was "as funny as a brick ship." A friend giggled with delight at the conception, and repeated it to others; but to his dismay he could find none who would enjoy it. "A brick ship!" they repeated. "That isn't funny; it's simply foolish." At another time, Bierce announced that he regarded every married man as his natural enemy; and the Philistines raved, saying he was evil, nasty, and a hopeless beast. The boyish fun of his remarks seemed always lost on the crowd. Again, when the missing-word nonsense was going on, he began to say obscure things, in his column, about a poem which Dr. David Starr Jordan had just published. At length he inaugurated a missing-word contest of his own, somewhat as follows: "Dr. Jordan is a ——, and a ——, and a ——." He invited the public to send him its guesses. Heaven knows what replies he received; but the Professor was worried, and asked Bierce's friends why the writer was getting after him. Finally the missing words were supplied: "Dr. Jordan is a gentleman, and a scholar, and a poet." Bierce supplied and published them himself.

Once a lawyer, whose remarkable name was Otto Tum Suden, broke out with some public matter that Bierce didn't like. Accordingly, he wrote a little jingle about Tum Suden, the burthen of which was "Tum Suden, tum duden, tum dey!" It completely silenced poor Tum.

It is not unnatural, however, that Bierce should have been misunderstood, and people always were misunderstanding him. Standing, one day, with a friend, on a high elevation at a midwinter fair, he looked down at a vast crowd swarming and sweating far below him. Suddnly, coming out of a reverie, he said: "Wouldn't it be fun to turn loose a

machine gun into that crowd!" He added a swift
and droll picture of the result, which sent his friend
into convulsions, the latter knowing perfectly well
that Bierce would not have harmed a single hair on
a head in that swarm. But suppose his friend had
been no friend at all — had just met the writer, and
did not know him for what he was! That was
Bierce's way, however, and it ran into print. People could never understand him — some people.

Even his friends did not escape his lash. However deep his affection for them, he never spared
them in public if they stepped awry. But they were
inclined to think it an honor when he got after them
in print, and, naturally, there was an admiring literary coterie that hailed him as master. I suspect
they flattered him, although I cannot imagine him
accepting their flattery. And he *was* a Master.
One of this group, perhaps the closest of his literary
friends, once sent him a story for criticism. Bierce
returned it with the laconic remark that his friend
"must have written it for the *Waverly Magazine*
when he was a school-girl."

Among his friends and pupils were the poets,
George Sterling and Herman Scheffauer, and he
was on the best of terms with the Bohemian crowd
that made old San Francisco a sort of American
Bagdad; but I believe he never participated in their
café dinners, where they were gazed at and mar-
veled over by the fringing crowd. He was uncon-

scious of his own greatness, in any offensive sense, and either ignored or failed to see the startled or admiring looks given him when people were told, "'That is Ambrose Bierce." He was not a showman. I have heard it said that women adored him, for he was cavalierly handsome; but he was not much of a ladies' man. As I have suggested, however, he was always a gentleman and gentlemen are none too plentiful.

An especially interesting chapter in his journalistic career began in 1896, when a great fight was being waged in the nation's capital. The late Collis P. Huntington was conducting a powerful lobby to pass his "refunding bill," releasing him and his associates of the Central Pacific Railroad from their obligations to the government. Bierce was asked by William Randolph Hearst to go to Washington for the *Examiner*, to give what aid he might in defeating the scheme. A Washington newspaper man said to Huntington: "Bierce is in town."

"How much does he want?" cynically asked Huntington.

This insult was reported to Bierce, who replied: "Please go back and tell him that my price is about seventy-five million dollars. If, when he is ready to pay, I happen to be out of town, he may hand it to my friend, the Treasurer of the United States."

The contest was notable. As in the Eugénie case, Bierce was in his element. He wrote so fast and so furiously that it became a whimsical saying that he wrote with a specially prepared pencil, because his pens became red hot and his ink boiled. The result was happy, whatever he used, for he drove the corruptionist gang out of the Capitol, and forced a withdrawal of the insolent measure. It was not so long ago that the last installment of the entire debt was handed to Bierce's "friend," the Treasurer of the United States.

Later, Bierce removed to Washington, where he spent his last years. He was already a celebrity when he came there to live, and was more or less of a lion; but his anger always was great when he fancied anyone was showing him off. It is said that he indignantly declined to attend a theater with a friend, in New York, because seats had been procured in a box for the party that was to accompany them. Another story tells of an alleged scene he made in a Washington drawing-room, when his host presented a street railway magnate. The car baron extended his hand.

"No!' thundered Bierce, in magnificent rage. "I wouldn't take your black hand for all the money you could steal in the next ten years! I ride in one of your cars every night and always am compelled to stand — there's never a seat for me."

And the story goes that the black hand was speedily withdrawn. I do not vouch for the tale; but it sounds a bit tru-ish, if not entirely so.

It has been remarked time and again that Bierce was embittered by failure of the world to appreciate his work, by his "obscurity." That is untrue. Recognition was slow, but he was certainly not unknown; indeed if a multiplicity of attacks upon a man may make him famous, Bierce was famous. It is the critics who are to blame for this myth; many attacked him, and many, eager to help him, spoke mournfully of his great and unappreciated genius; and after a time the story stuck. In a breezy jingle, Bierce himself summed up this aspect of the case, as follows:

My, how my fame rings out in every zone —
A thousand critics shouting, "He's unknown!"

It is probably true, also, that the foreword to his first book of stories, *Tales of Soldiers and Civilians,* had something to do with the legend:

> Denied existence by the chief publishing houses of the country, this book owes itself to Mr. E. L. G. Steele, merchant, of this city [San Francisco]. In attesting Mr. Steele's faith in his judgment and his friend, it will serve its author's main and best ambition.

But, as the years went by, the *cognoscenti* came to know him very well indeed. And those who knew him best, in his later years, assert that he was not morose and unhappy, although he was a considerable sufferer from asthma, and had tried various climates without result.

Despite all his scoffings at clergymen and church

folk, and despite his so-called heterodox opinions, Bierce made profession of a profound Christian faith. Even so, the orthodox will frown at it, but the man who wrote so exalted a tribute to Jesus of Nazareth could hardly have been the hopeless agnostic he was often pictured.

"This is my ultimate and determinate sense of right," he wrote. " 'What under the circumstances would Christ have done?' — the Christ of the New Testament, not the Christ of the commentators, theologians, priests, and parsons."

And his friend, Edwin Markham, said of him:

"He is a composite mind — a blending of Hafiz the Persian, Swift, Poe, Thoreau, with sometimes a gleam of the Galilean."

II. THE MASTER

It seems likely that the enduring fame of the most remarkable man, in many ways, of his day, will be founded chiefly upon his stories of war — the blinding flashes of revelation and interpretation that make up the group under the laconic legend, "Soldier," in his greatest book, *In the Midst of Life.* In these are War, stripped of pageantry and glamor, stark in naked realism, terrible in grewsome fascination, yet of a sinister beauty. Specifically, it is the American Civil War that furnishes his characters and his texts, the great internecine conflict throughout which he gallantly fought; but it is War of which he writes, the hideous Thing.

Perhaps it is the attraction of repulsion that, again and again, leads one to these tales — although there is a record of a man who, having read them once, would not repeat the experiment — but it is that only in part. There is more than mere terror in them; there is religion and poetry, and much of the traditional beauty of battle. Their author was both soldier and poet, and in the war stories of Ambrose Bierce, the horror and ugliness, the lure and loveliness of war are so blended that there seems no distinct line of demarcation; the dividing line is not a point or sign, but a penumbra. Over the whole broods an occult significance that transcends experience.

Outstanding, even in so collectively remarkable a group, are three stories, "A Horseman in the Sky," "A Son of the Gods," and "Chickamauga." The first mentioned quietly opens with a young soldier, a Federal sentry, on duty at a point in the mountains overlooking a wooded drop of a thousand feet. He is a Virginian who has conceived it his duty to join the forces of the North, and who thus finds himself in arms against his family. It is imperative that the position of the camp guarded by the young soldier be kept secret; yet he is asleep at his post. Waking, he looks across the gorge, and on the opposite height beholds a magnificent equestrian statue — a Confederate officer on horseback, calmly surveying the camp beneath.

The young soldier, unobserved by his enemy, aims at the officer's breast. But suddenly his soul is in tumult; he is shaken by convulsive shudders. He cannot take life in that way. If only the officer would see him and offer battle! Then he recalls his father's admonition at their parting: at whatever cost he must do his duty. The horseman in gray turns his head. His features are easily discernible now. There is a pause. Then the young soldier shifts his aim from the officer's breast and, with stony calm, fires at the horse. A moment later, a Federal officer, some distance down the side of the cliff, sees an amazing thing — a man on horseback, riding down into the valley through the air.

Here is the conclusion to that story:

Ten minutes had hardly passed when a Federal sergeant crept cautiously to him on hands and knees. Druse neither turned his head nor looked at him, but lay without motion or sign of recognition.

"Did you fire?" the sergeant whispered.

"Yes."

"At what?"

"A horse. It was standing on yonder rock — pretty far out. You see it is no longer there. It went over the cliff."

The man's face was white but he showed no other sign of emotion. Having answered, he turned away his face and said no more. The sergeant did not understand.

"See here, Druse," he said, after a moment's silence, "it's no use making a mystery. I order you to report. Was there anybody on the horse?"

"Yes."

"Who?"

"My father."

The sergeant rose to his feet and walked away. "Good God!" he said.

It may be claimed that the *idea* of this story — its conclusion — is not original with Bierce. I don't know, although for all anyone can say to the contrary the episode may be a transcript from life. Certainly, in this form it is original enough. De Maupassant contrives the same sense of "shock" in the tale of a sailor who, after years of wandering, returns to the village to find his old home vanished, and who, in consequence, betakes himself to a shadier section of town. In the midst of his maudlin carousing, he discovers in the half-naked creature he is fondling, his sister. Remotely, the idea is the same in both stories, and, I fancy, it antedates De Maupassant by hundreds of years. *Since* publication of Bierce's tale, young writers in numbers deliberately have sought the effect (Peccavi!) with tales that are strangely reminiscent; and Billy Sunday rhetorically tells a "true story" of the same sort, which might have been taken directly from the French master. Thus does life plagiarize from literature, in later days, after literature first has plagiarized from life.

At any rate, it is a situation that was never better handled, an idea never more cleanly distorted, than by Bierce. "A Horseman in the Sky" is one of the most effective of his astonishing vignettes, and is given first place in the volume. It has one objection, which applies to all terror, horror, and mystery tales; once read, the secret is out, and rereading cannot recapture the first *story* thrill. It may be, however, that all literature, of whatever classification, is open to the same objection. Fortunately, as in

the case of Bierce, there is more to literature than
the mere "story."

There is less of this *story* in "A Son of the Gods,"
but as a shining glimpse of the tragic beauty of battle it is, I believe, unique; possibly it is Bierce's
finest achievement in the art of *writing*. He calls it
a "study in the historical present tense." In order
to spare the lives of the skirmishers, a young staff
officer rides forward toward the crest of a bare ridge
crowned with a stone wall, to make the enemy dis-
close himself, if the enemy is there. The enemy *is*
there and, being discovered, has no further reason
for concealment. The doomed officer, instead of
retreating to his friends, rides parallel to the wall,
in a hail of rifle fire, and thence obliquely to other
ridges, to uncover other concealed batteries and
regiments. . .

The dust drifts away. Incredible! — that
enchanted horse and rider have passed a ravine
and are climbing another slope to unveil another conspiracy of silence, to thwart the will
of another armed host. Another moment and
that crest too is in eruption. The horse rears
and strikes the air with its forefeet. They are
down at last. But look again — the man has
detached himself from the dead animal. He
stands erect, motionless, holding his sabre in his
right hand straight above his head. His face is
toward us. Now he lowers his hand to a level
with his face and moves it outward, the blade
of the sabre describing a downward curve. It

is a sign to us, to the world, to posterity.   It is
a hero's salute to death and history.

Again the spell is broken; our men attempt
to cheer; they are choking with emotion; they
utter hoarse, discordant cries; they clutch their
weapons and press tumultuously forward into
the open.   The skirmishers, without orders,
against orders, are going forward at a keen
run, like hounds unleashed.   Our cannon speak
and the enemy's now open in full chorus; to
right and left as far as we can see, the distant
crest, seeming now so near, erects its towers of
cloud, and the great shot pitch roaring down
among our moving masses.   Flag after flag of
ours emerges from the wood, line after line
sweeps forth, catching the sunlight on its bur-
nished arms.   .   .

Bierce has been called a Martian; a man who
loved war.   In a way, I think he did; he was a born
fighter, and he fought, as later he wrote, with a
suave fierceness, deadly, direct, and unhastening.
He was also an humane and tender spirit.   As typical as the foregoing paragraphs are the following
lines, with which the narrative concludes:

The skirmishers return, gathering up the
dead.   Ah, those many, many needless dead!
That great soul whose beautiful body is lying
over yonder, so conspicuous against the sere hill-
side — could it not have been spared the bitter
consciousness of a vain devotion?   Would one
exception have marred too much the pitiless
perfection of the divine, eternal plan?

In his more genuinely *horrible* vein, "Chickamauga" is unrivaled; a grotesquely shocking account
of a deaf-mute child who, wandering from home,
encountered in the woods a host of wounded soldiers hideously crawling from the battlefield, and
thought they were playing a game. Rebuffed by the
jawless man, upon whose back he tried to ride, the
child ultimately returns to his home, to find it
burned and his mother slain and horribly mutilated
by a shell. There is nothing occult in this story,
but, with others of its *genre*, it probes the very
depths of material horror.

"An Occurrence at Owl Creek Bridge" is better
known than many of Bierce's tales, and here again
is a form that has attracted imitators. Like a pan-
toum, the conclusion brings the narrative back to
its beginning. A man is engaged in being hanged,
in this extraordinary tale, and preparations are pro-
ceeding in a calm and businesslike manner. An order is given, and the man is dropped.

Consciousness returns, and he feels the water
about him; the rope has broken, he knows, and he
has fallen into the stream. He is fired upon, but
escapes. After days of travel and incredible hard-
ship, he reaches his home. His wife is in the door-
way to greet him, and he springs forward with extended arms. At that instant, he feels a stunning
blow on the back of his neck, a blaze of light is
about him — then darkness and silence. "Peyton

Farquhar was dead; his body, with a broken neck, swung gently from side to side beneath the timbers of the Owl Creek bridge."

Again there is the sense of shock, at the end, as we realize that between the instant of the hanged man's drop and the succeeding instant of his death, he has lived days of emotion and suspense. .

The tales of civilians, which make up the second half of Bierce's greatest book, are of a piece with his war stories. Probably nothing more weirdly awful has been conceived than such tales as "A Watcher by the Dead," "The Man and the Snake," and "The Boarded Window," unless it be Stevenson's "The Body Snatcher." The volume entitled *Can Such Things Be?* contains several similar stories, although, as a whole, it is apocryphal. In "The Mocking Bird" we find again the *motif* of "A Horseman in the Sky;" in "The Death of Halpin Frayser" there is a haunting detail and a grewsome imagery that suggest Poe, and in "My Favorite Murder," one of the best tales Bierce ever wrote, there is a satirical whimsicality and a cynical brutality that make the tale an authentic masterpiece of *something* — perhaps humor!

"A literary quality that is a consecration," remarked one critic, of Bierce's method and method-results. That is better than speaking of his "style," for I think the miracle of Bierce's fascination is as much a lack of what is called *style* as anything else.

The clarity and directness of his thought and expression, and the nervous strength and purity of his diction, are the most unmistakable characteristics of his manner.

Bierce the satirist is seen in nearly all of his stories, but in *Fantastic Fables*, and *The Devil's Dictionary* we have satire bereft of romantic association; the keenest satire since Swift, glittering, bitter, venomous, but thoroughly honest. His thrusts are at and through the heart of sham. A beautiful specimen of his temper is the following fable:

An Associate Justice of the Supreme Court was sitting by a river when a traveler approached and said:

"I wish to cross. Would it be lawful to use this boat?"

"It would," was the reply, "it is my boat."

The traveler thanked him, and pushing the boat into the water, embarked and rowed away. But the boat sank and he was drowned.

"Heartless man!" said an Indignant Spectator, "why did you not tell him that your boat had a hole in it?"

"The matter of the boat's condition," said the great jurist, "was not brought before me."

The same cynical humor is revealed in the introductory paragraphs of the story already referred to, called "My Favorite Murder." The solemn absurdities of the law were Bierce's frequent target; thus, in his *Devil's Dictionary*, the definition of the phrase "court fool" is, laconically, "the plain-tiff." His biting wit is nowhere better evidenced than in this mocking lexicon. Bacchus, he conceives to be "a convenient deity invented by the ancients as an excuse for getting drunk;" and a Prelate is "a church officer having a superior degree of holi-ness and a fat preferment. One of Heaven's aris-tocracy. A gentleman of God." More humor-ously, a Garter is "an elastic band intended to keep a woman from coming out of her stockings and des-olating the country."

In the same key are his collected epigrams, in which we learn that "woman would be more charm-ing if one could fall into her arms without falling into her hands."

With all forms of literary expression, Bierce ex-perimented successfully; but in verse his percentage of permanent contributions is smaller than in any other department. His output, while enormous, was for the most part ephemeral, and the wisdom of collecting even the least of his jingles may well be called into question. At least half of the hun-dreds of verses contained in the two volumes of his collected works given over to poetry, might have been left for collectors to discover and resurrect; and some delightful volumes of *juvenilia* and *ana* thus might have been posthumously achieved for him by the collecting fraternity. But, "someone will surely search them out and put them into circula-

tion," said their author, in defense of their publication in the definitive edition, and there they are, the
good, the bad, and the indifferent.

Happily, in the ocean of newspaper jingles and
rhymed quips there is much excellent poetry. Kip-
ling, by some, is asserted to have derived his "Re-
cessional" from Bierce's "Invocation," a noble and
stately poem; and in "The Passing Show," "Finis
Æternitatis," and some of the sonnets we have
poetry of a high order. Maugre, we have much
excellent satire in many of his journalistic rhymes.
Like Swift and Butler, and Pope and Byron, Bierce
gibbeted a great many nobodies; but, as he himself
remarks, "satire, like other arts, is its own excuse,
and is not dependent for its interest on the person-
ality of those who supply the occasion for it." If
many of Bierce's *Black Beetles in Amber* seem
flat, many too are as virile and keen as when they
were written; and if he flayed men alive, just as
certainly he raised the moral tone of the community
he dominated in a manner the value of which is
perhaps measureless.

The best example of poetry, however, left us by
Bierce, *me judice*, is that great prose poem, *The
Monk and the Hangman's Daughter*. This work
is the joint production of Bierce and G. Adolphe
Danziger. The latter translated it from the Ger-
man of Prof. Richard Voss and, I believe, elaborated it. Being unsure of his English, Danziger

gave it over to Bierce for revision. Bierce, too, elaborated it, practically rewriting it, he testified, as well as changing it materially. There was discussion about authorship honors; but the book is a bit of literary art that is a credit to all three men, and that would be a credit to six. The world would be poorer without this delicate and lovely romance. Saturated with the color and spirit of the mediæval days it depicts, it is as authentic a classic as *Aucassin and Nicolette*; and its *denouement* is as terrible as it is beautiful. The strange story of Ambrosius the monk, and the outcast girl Benedicta, "the hangman's daughter," is one of the masterpieces of literature.

Ambrose Bierce was a great writer and a great man. He was a great master of English; but it is difficult to place him. He is possibly the most versatile genius in American letters. He is the equal of Stevenson in weird, shadowy effect, and in expression he is Stevenson's superior. Those who compare his work with that of Stephen Crane (in his war stories) have not read him understandingly. Crane was a fine and original genius, but he was, and is, the pupil where Bierce is Master. Bierce's "style" is simpler and less spasmodic than Crane's, and Bierce brought to his labor a first-hand knowledge of war, and an imagination more terrible even than that which gave us *The Red Badge of Courage*. The horrors of both men sometimes transcend artistic effect; but their works are enduring peace tracts.

It has been said that Bierce's stories are "formula," and it is in a measure true; but the formula is that of a master chemist, and it is inimitable. He set the pace for the throng of satirical fabulists who have since written; and his essays, of which nothing has been said, are powerful, of immense range, and of impeccable diction. His influence on the writers of his time, while unacknowledged, is wide. Rarely did he attempt anything sustained; his work is composed of keen, darting fragments. His only novel is a redaction. But who shall complain, when his fragments are so perfect?

III. THE MYSTERY

In the fall of the year 1913, Ambrose Bierce, being then some months past his seventy-first birthday anniversary, started for Mexico. He had for some time, and with keen interest, followed the fortunes of the revolutionary cause headed by Francisco Villa; and he believed that cause a just one. From various points along the line of his journey, before he reached the southern republic, Bierce wrote to his friends. In December of 1913 the last letter he is known to have written was received by his daughter. It was dated the month of its receipt, and from Chihuahua, Mexico. In it Bierce mentioned, casually enough, that he had attached himself, unofficially, to a division of Villa's army — the exact capacity of his service is not known — and spoke of a prospective advance on Ojinaga. The rest is silence.

No further word, bearing the unmistakable stamp of authenticity, ever has come out of Mexico. There have been rumors without number, even long categorical accounts of his death at the hands of the revolutionists, but all must be called false. There is in them not the faintest ring of truth. They rep-

resent merely the inevitable speculation, and the inevitable "fakes" of unscrupulous correspondents.
Typical of the innumerable "clews" offered is the
following: One newspaper correspondent in El
Paso reported that a second correspondent had told
him that he (the second correspondent) had seen
and talked with Bierce before the author passed into
Mexico; that Bierce had declared he would offer
his services to the revolutionary cause, and that,
failing to make such a connection, he would "crawl
into some out-of-the-way hole in the mountains and
die." The author of these pages hastily communi-
cated with the second correspondent, and the second
correspondent, in a positive communication, vowed
that he had never seen Bierce, nor had he heard the
story of Bierce's reported utterance.

The most elaborate account of Bierce's "death"
was quoted in full from the *Mexican Review*, by
the *Washington Post*, under date of April 27, 1919.
Its extraordinary detail gives it a semblance of
truth that other accounts have lacked, and, without
intending to perpetuate a story which Bierce's
friends and relatives do not for a moment believe, I
reproduce it in its ungrammatical entirety:

A short time since the *Review* editor was
conversing with a friend, a former officer in the
constitutionalist army, and casually asked him
if he had ever heard of an American named
Ambrose Bierce. To his surprise he replied

that he had met him several times and had become quite well acquainted with him. This was due to the fact that Bierce could speak little if any Spanish, while the officer is well educated and speaks English fluently.

The latter declared that he saw and talked with Bierce several times in the vicinity of Chihuahua late in 1913 or early in 1914. Later — 1915 — he met a sergeant of Villa's army, an old acquaintance, and this man told him about having witnessed the execution of an American who corresponded in every manner with Bierce's description.

This affair took place near Icamole, a village in the region of Monterey and Saltillo, east of Chihuahua state, in August, 1915. The constitutionalists occupied that village while Gen. Tomas Urbina, one of Villa's most bloodthirsty fellows, was nearby and between that place and the border.

One day an American, accompanied by a Mexican, convoying four mules, on one of which was a machine gun, while the others were loaded with ammunition, was captured on the trail, headed toward Icamole, and taken before Urbina. The Mexican told Urbina that he had been engaged by another Mexican to guide the mules and the American to the constitutionalist camp at Icamole. That was all he knew. The American apparently could not speak or understand any Spanish, and made no intelligent reply to the questions asked him.

The bloodthirsty Urbina, who was never so happy as when killing some one himself or ordering it to be done, wearied of questioning the prisoners and ordered them to be shot at once.

The two were stood up in front of a firing squad, where the Mexican threw himself on his knees, stretched out his arms, and refused to have his eyes bandaged, saying he wanted to "see himself killed." All he asked was that his face be not mutilated, which was not done.

Seeing his companion on his knees, the American followed suit, but the Mexican told him to stand up. He did not understand what was said, but remained on his knees, arms outstretched, like his companion, and with unbandaged eyes he met his death at the hands of the firing squad. The two victims were buried by the side of the trail.

The sergeant who witnessed the affair described Bierce exactly, though he had never seen him to his knowledge. Incidentally it may be stated that Urbina himself soon after met his death by Villa's orders at the hands of the notorious "Matador Fierro."

It is to be doubted whether Villa ever knew about this double execution, such affairs being common enough at that time.

Inquiry is now being made for the sergeant in question, in order that further details of the affair may be secured, as well as information regarding the exact locality of the execution and the burial place of the two victims.

Only two things need to be considered in refuting the foregoing narrative. First, this is only one of a great many stories, despite its painstaking vraisemblance; and, second, the execution is dated in the fall of 1915, approximately two years after Bierce's last letter. Had Ambrose Bierce been alive in 1915, had he been living at almost any time between the date of his last letter and the reported date of his death, he would have sent some communication to his friends and relatives. This is recognized by all who knew him best, and is the final answer to the extravagant chronicle in the *Mexican Review*. It may be remarked, however, in passing, that the carefully detailed account is just such a tale as might have been constructed by a press agent eager to lift the onus of Bierce's disappearance from official Mexican shoulders; and of such paid press agents there have been many. It will be noted that care is taken to report also the execution of Urbina, and even to "whitewash" Villa, although I believe the propaganda to have been Carranzista.

This careful piece of imagination was followed closely by a still more carefully elaborated account of the same story. Written by James H. Wilkins, it appeared in the *San Francisco Bulletin* of March 24, 1920. Wilkins quotes George F. Weeks, who was probably responsible for the former story, since he was editor of the *Mexican Review,* speaks of Major Bierce as having been military advisor to Carranza, and dwells at length on Bierce's alleged expressed desire to "die in battle." One Edmundo Melero, an associate editor of the *Mexican Review,* is declared to have been with Bierce almost from the moment of his arrival in Mexico, but as Melero died of pneumonia the day after Wilkins arrived in Mexico City (I am quoting Wilkins's story), Wilkins could not interview him. Fortunately, Weeks knew all that Melero could have told, and Weeks told Wilkins that Melero had been seeking a Mexican, then in Mexico City, who had been present at the attack on the mule train when Bierce was "captured" and "executed."

To find this Indian in a city of a million souls was no trick for Wilkins, and the discovered eye-witness repeated the story I have already quoted, with unimportant variations. The convenient Indian then produced a *photograph* of Ambrose Bierce, which had been among the effects taken from the "body." Wilkins identified it at once. But the Indian would not part with it; he preferred to destroy the photograph, believing it had served its purpose, and fearing consequences to himself when the Wilkins revelation was published. This photograph was the sensation of the Wilkins story, which otherwise was the same story as formerly told.

A friend of mine in California fairly rushed this article to me, saying, "Wilkins is an old and reliable journalist." I shall not attempt to deny either his age or his reliability, but I will casually suggest -

that *if* he is reliable he is extraordinarily gullible, whatever his age.

One remarkable story came privately to me, and was to the positive effect that Ambrose Bierce had been alive and well in San Luis Potosi, as late as December of 1918, five years after his disappearance and after his last letter to his friends. The narrator of that tale believed him to be still living (May, 1920), and ready to come back and astound the world when his "death" had been sufficiently advertised. There were many details to the story, and another Mexican figured. This Mexican had seen a portrait of Bierce in the story-teller's office, had exclaimed at sight of it, and had told of knowing the original; Bierce and this Indian, it developed, had parted company in San Luis Potosi in December of 1918! The Major was known to the Mexican as "Don Ambrosio." But *this* Mexican was murdered in Los Angeles, in a triangular love scrape, as was attested surely enough by a newspaper account of his murder, so the narrator's chief witness had vanished. This investigator, too, was, at least, too credible; although he was shrewd enough to see through the Weeks and Wilkins stories, and to tear them to pieces. Certainly he knew better than to accuse Bierce of seeking morbid publicity.

Other extraordinary tales there have been, and a dispatch to the *New York World* of April 3, 1915, dated from Bloomington, Illinois, soberly recited that Mrs. H. D. Cowden of that city, Bierce's daughter, had received a letter from her father which entirely cleared the mystery of his disappearance. He was even then in France, it seemed, an officer on Lord Kitchener's staff, had escaped injury, and was in good health. Yet from Mrs. Cowden's own lips I have had it that no such letter, no such information conveyed in whatever manner, had ever reached her. A later story reported that Bierce had perished with Kitchener, when the great soldier was drowned.

This is all sensational journalism. There is every reason to doubt that Bierce ever left Mexico; that he long survived his last bit of letter-writing — the brief communication to his daughter, in December of 1913. The manner of his passing probably never will be known, but it is to be recalled that he suffered from asthma, and that he was more than seventy-one years of age when he went away. Were he alive in the year 1920 he would be 78 years old.

There is one further consideration: Did Bierce, when he went into Mexico, expect to return? Did he go, calmly and deliberatly, to his death? Did he, indeed, seek death? The question has been raised, and so it must be answered. In support of the contention, two highly significant letters have been offered. These were received by Mrs. Josephine Clifford McCrackin of San José, California, long a warm friend of the vanished author, and there is not the slightest doubt of their authenticity. The first, chronologically, is dated from Washington, September 10, 1913, and is as follows:

Dear Joe: The reason that I did not answer your letter sooner is — I have been away (in New York) and did not have it with me. I suppose I shall not see your book for a long time, for I am going away and have no notion when I shall return. I expect to go to, perhaps across, South America — possibly via Mexico, if I can get through without being stood up against a wall and shot as a gringo. But that is better than dying in bed, is it not? If Dunc did not need you so badly I'd ask you to get your hat and come along. God bless and keep you.

The faint suggestion in this letter is more clearly defined in the second and last letter received by Mrs. McCrackin, three days later:

Dear Joe: Thank you for the book. I thank you for your friendship — and much besides. This is to say good-by at the end of a pleasant correspondence in which your woman's prerogative of having the last word is denied to you. Before I could receive it I shall be gone. But some time, somewhere, I hope to hear from you again. Yes, I shall go into Mexico with a pretty definite purpose, which, however, is not at present disclosable. You must try to forgive my obstinacy in not "perishing" where I am. I want to be where something worth while is going on, or where nothing whatever is going on. Most of what is going on in your own country is exceedingly distasteful to me.

Pray for me? Why, yes, dear — that will not harm either of us. I loathe religions, a Christian gives me qualms and a Catholic sets my teeth on edge, but pray for me just the same, for with all those faults upon your head (it's a nice head, too), I am pretty fond of you, I guess. May you live as long as you want to, and then pass smilingly into the darkness — the good, good darkness. Devotedly your friend.

He goes "with a pretty definite purpose;" his "obstinacy" will not allow him to perish in Washington, and death at the hands of the Mexicans is "better than dying in bed." He wishes to be where something worth while is going on, or "where nothing whatever is going on;" and, finally, there is the reference to the "good, good darkness."

Yet also he had announced his intention, if possible, to cross South America.

It is difficult to get away from the hints in those two letters; and the assumption that Bierce knew he would not return is inescapable. But to assume that he cordially sought death is another matter. He would be ready for it when it came, he would pass smilingly into the "good, good darkness," but does anyone who knows Ambrose Bierce or his work suppose that he would encourage, let us say, his own murder? That he would rush into battle, let us say, hoping for a friendly bullet through his heart?

That his passing was, in effect, a suicide, although the hand may have been another than his own? Ambrose Bierce's friends do not think so, and they are right. His "good-by" to his friends was real enough, but all he certainly knew was that somewhere, some time, perhaps in a few months, perhaps in a year or two, death would overtake him, and that he would not have returned to his home. That death did come to him, not long after he wrote the last letter received by his daughter, we must believe.

If he was murdered by bandits, and had a chance for life, it is safe to assume that there was a fight. If he died of disease, which is not at all improbable, he regretted his inability to write. Bierce was not cruel to his friends.

It is likely that the disappearance is complete, that the mystery never will be solved. The United States government's investigation has come to nothing, and indeed it has been lax enough.

Ambrose Bierce was born in Meiggs County, Ohio, June 24, 1842, son of Marcus Aurelius and Laura (Sherwood) Bierce. He died — where? And when? Or is he dead? The time for hope would seem to have passed. One thinks of that grim prophecy, years ago; and there has been no wireless.

Setting aside the grief of friends and relatives, there is something terribly beautiful and fitting in the manner of the passing of Ambrose Bierce; a tragically appropriate conclusion to a life of erratic adventure and high endeavor. Soldier-fighter and soldier-writer. Scotson Clark's well-known caricature of Bierce dragging a pen from a scabbard is the undying portrait of the man.

CPSIA information can be obtained
at www.ICGtesting.com
Printed in the USA
LVOW10s1010080717
540672LV00011B/962/P

9 781331 995142